LEARN
ABOUT

Strange Animals

Edited by Belinda Gallagher
Cover design by Oxprint Ltd.

ISBN 0 86112 722 6

Published by Brimax Books Ltd, Newmarket, England 1991.
Printed in Hong Kong.

LEARN ABOUT

Strange Animals

Written by Jane and David Glover
Illustrated by Brian Watson

Brimax · Newmarket · England

Animals can seem strange if their lives are very different from ours. They may live in odd places, eat unusual food or have strange bodies.

The Darwin frog keeps its eggs in its mouth. The tadpoles do not jump out until they have changed into tiny frogs.

The golden mole doesn't have any eyes. It lives underground in the dark.

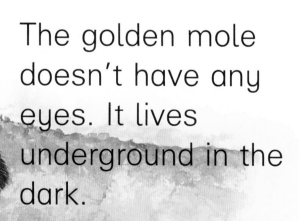

The aardvark eats termites. It has big ears to listen for them moving inside their mounds, strong claws to dig them out and a long tongue to lick them up.

Thorny devils and porcupines have spikes to protect their bodies. If a porcupine is attacked it turns around, points its sharp quills at its enemy, and charges backwards.

Some of the strangest looking animals live deep in the ocean. There is very little light thousands of feet below the water's surface, so many of the animals that live here glow in the dark.

Giant squid can grow up to 50 feet (16 m) in length – longer than a bus. They have ten tentacles and hunt large fish. They can move very quickly, not by swimming, but by squirting water from their bodies like jet engines.

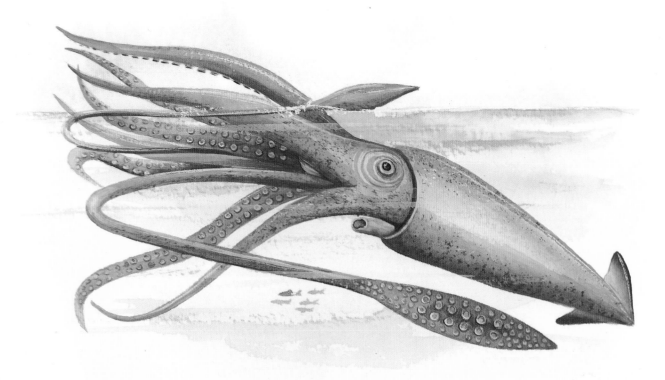

Gulper eels swim along with their huge mouths wide open collecting food from the water.

The football fish has a round body covered in bony plates. It has a small light attached to a long spine, which floats above its head. This light attracts other fish, which the football fish then eats.

Some fish can make electricity with their bodies.

The cat fish can give an electric shock to an enemy to frighten it away.

The electric eel is even more powerful than the cat fish. It uses electricity to stun its prey. Its electric shock can knock a man over if he touches it in the water.

Nobody really knows why the hammer head shark has such a funny shaped head. One reason could be that having widely spaced nostrils helps it find its prey by smell.

River dolphins are almost completely blind. The water they live in is so muddy, they do not need their eyesight. Instead, they find their way around by making sounds and listening for echoes.

Sea anemones may look like plants but they are in fact animals. Some of the most beautiful anemones live on coral reefs. They catch small fish in their stinging tentacles.

Clown fish are covered in a special slime to protect them from the sea anemones' stings. They live safely within the anemones' tentacles and are protected from fish which might eat them.

Sea cucumbers are really animals, too. They come in many different sizes. They trap tiny pieces of food in the tentacles around their mouths.

When the puffer fish is attacked, it gulps in lots of water and puffs itself up into a huge ball. This makes it look very fierce to its enemies. Its sharp spines also make it difficult to swallow.

Lung fish live in rivers and swamps. In the dry season they bury themselves in the mud. They can stay underground for months, or even years, waiting for the rains to come again.

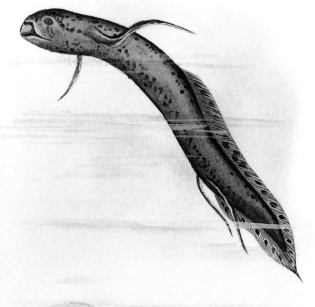

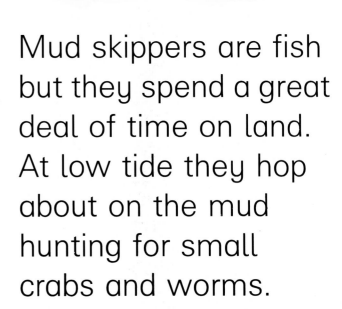

Mud skippers are fish but they spend a great deal of time on land. At low tide they hop about on the mud hunting for small crabs and worms.

Spadefoot toads live in the desert. They bury themselves in the sand so they don't dry out. When there is heavy rain, spadefoot toads lay their eggs in puddles. The tadpoles must hatch and grow quickly before the water dries up.

The spring salamander is an amphibian. This means it can live on land but must return to water to breed. The spring salamander spends most of its life in rock pools and springs, but on rainy nights it may come onto land to look for food.

The duck-billed platypus and the spiny anteater are furry mammals like cats and dogs but they lay eggs like birds.

The spiny ant-eater has strong feet for digging and a long sticky tongue for licking up ants. The female keeps her egg in a special pouch. It hatches after 7–10 days. The baby stays in the pouch feeding on its mother's milk for another six weeks.

The female duck-billed platypus lays her eggs in a burrow lined with damp leaves. When they hatch, the babies are naked and blind. They stay in the nest until their waterproof fur has grown.

The duck-billed platypus feeds under water. It has webbed feet and uses its bill to search for worms and insects on the river bed.

The giant armadillo is about 3 feet (1 m) long and can weigh as much as a man. It uses its powerful claws for making burrows and digging up termite nests.

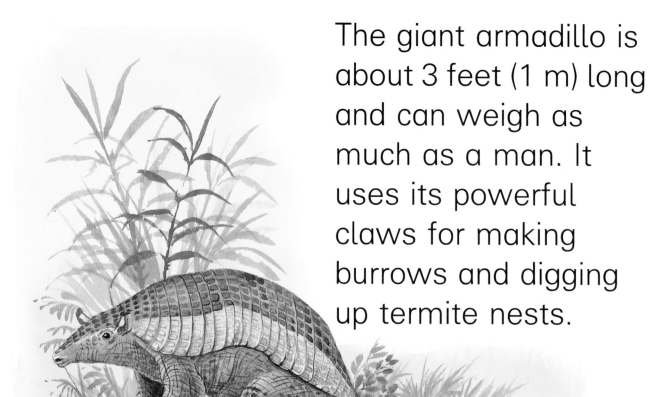

The nine-banded armadillo can roll into a tight ball if it is frightened. It is covered in bony plates which act as protection. These keep its body safe from enemies. The female nine-banded armadillo usually has 4 identical babies at one time.

Pangolins are protected by horny scales which overlap like tiles on a roof.

Naked mole-rats have just a few long hairs to help them feel their way underground. They live in colonies like bees in a hive. There are workers which dig the tunnels and collect food, and a 'queen' which has all the babies.

Bush babies and tarsiers feed at night. They have huge eyes and very good hearing to help them find insects. They use their long fingers to grip the branches as they jump from tree to tree.

The slow loris only moves very, very slowly. If it is frightened it keeps absolutely still until it feels safe again.

Flying lemurs glide from tree to tree by spreading folds of skin between their legs and their tail. During the day they sleep in holes. They come out at night to feed on leaves and fruit. The female carries her baby everywhere until it becomes too heavy.

There are more than a thousand different kinds of bat in the world. They are the only mammals that can truly fly.

The biggest bats are called flying foxes. Their wings can be as long as a swan's. They spend the day hanging upside down in jungle trees and caves. At dusk they take off in huge flocks to feed on fruit and flowers.

Smaller bats mainly eat insects, though some catch small birds, frogs and fish. They can find their prey at night by making sounds and listening for echoes. Many have strange looking faces and ears.

Vampire bats have very sharp teeth. They feed by biting a cow or horse while it sleeps and lapping up its blood.

Strange Animals quiz

Now you have read about strange animals, how many of these questions can you answer? Look back in the book for help if you need to.

True or false?

1. Some animals can make electricity.
2. The spiny ant-eater is a bird.
3. All bats eat insects.
4. Sea cucumbers are plants.
5. Golden moles can see in the dark.

What is it?

Can you name the following animals and tell what is strange about them?

6.

7.

8.

9.

Answers

1. True – the electric catfish and the electric eel can.
2. False – it is a mammal, but it lays an egg.
3. False – some bats eat fruit.
4. False – they are animals.
5. False – they do not have eyes.
6. Nine-banded armadillo – its body is covered in bony plates.
7. Duck-billed platypus – it is a mammal, but it lays eggs.
8. Puffer fish – it can puff its body up into a huge ball to frighten away enemies.
9. Vampire bat – it is the only bat that feeds on other animals' blood.